TOR MARK

Published 2019

ISBN 978 0 85025 456 3 Cornwall
ISBN 978 0 85025 455 6 Devon
ISBN 978 0 85025 457 0 Dorset

Published by Tor Mark,
United Downs Industrial Estate,
St Day, Redruth, Cornwall TR16 5HY

www.tormark.co.uk

Printed and bound in Great Britain
by Cambrian Printers

GOLD LEAF BOOKS

BAKING
RECIPES

CONTENTS

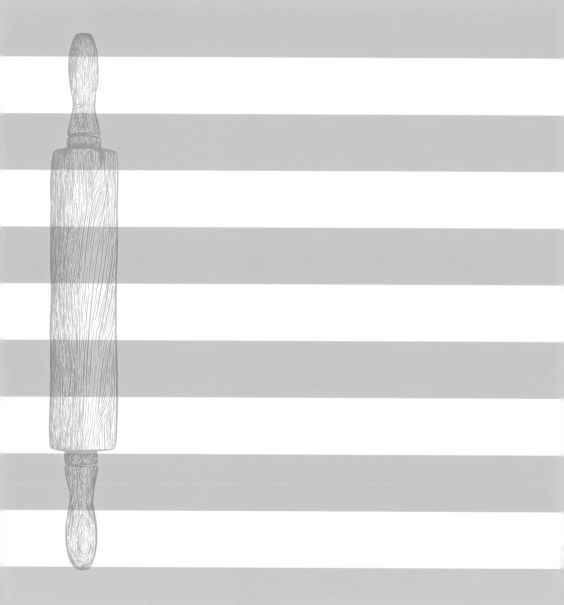

INTRODUCTION

Baking is for everyone! Whether you're new to cooking or have been practising for a long time, the secret is…give it a go! The absolute joy of baking is that there's always something delicious to eat at the end.

I am continuously inspired by the world around me. Visiting local farm shops, food halls and tea gardens is just as inspiring as popping into bakeries and coffee shops. Trying other people's baking is an absolute must; I find that bakers are delighted to talk about their baking, and this in itself gives me ideas for what to bake next.

If you are new to baking, start with a few simple bakes to get you going; Chocolate Crumbles or Lemon Syrup Cake are absolutely ideal for this. Once you're feeling a little more confident, think about the bakes you and your friends like best and experiment; ground almonds make an excellent substitute for self-raising flour (make sure your eaters are able to eat nuts) and gives a deeper texture that is quite delectable. Similarly, chopping your own stem ginger and using this instead of ground ginger will give your Gingerbread an altogether lighter taste.

A couple of things you may wish to think about are that I have an Aga and as such, my ovens are always hot. I have therefore assumed that you will always pre-heat your oven. I also grease my tins with butter thinking that butter's natural qualities really do encourage an extra-goodness to the flavours. Having said that, some of my friends prefer greasing and lining using baking parchment so it really is up to you! Cooking times are a guideline only, as this always depends on individual ovens. I suggest you use your nose – if something smells cooked, it usually is, regardless of the cooking time suggested.

I trust these recipes will inspire you as they have done me, and delight everyone you invite to share them. Enjoy!

Tamar Swift

APPLE CAKE · **APPLE** SHORTCAKE · **CHEESY** CAKES · **CHOCOLATE** OATCAKES · **CHRISTMAS** CAKE · **COFFEE & WALNUT** CAKE · **CUT & COME AGAIN** CAKE · **HEAVY** CAKE · **LEMON SYRUP** CAKE · **SYRUP CARROT** CAKE

CAKES

APPLE CAKE

This is the most delicious of cakes, moist and sweet but with a zing of flavour. Granny Smith eating apples are best but you could try a variety of apples to create a mix of texture & flavour.

SHOPPING LIST...

100g butter
100g caster sugar
1 large egg - *beaten*
½ tsp vanilla essence
200g self raising flour
1 eating apple - *thinly sliced*
milk to mix

Optional toppings:

1 eating apple - *sliced*
flaked almonds

Line a 20cm cake tin with baking parchment.

Cream the butter and sugar, add the beaten egg and the vanilla essence and mix well. Gradually fold in the sifted flour, apple and milk until you have a soft dropping consistency. Add a little more milk if necessary.

Bake the cake for approximately 40 minutes at 350-375°F/180-190°C, or until a skewer comes out clean. This is best eaten the same day.

Optional toppings: place the sliced apple and sprinkle flaked almonds on top.

APPLE SHORTCAKE

—◇—

You'll need a fairly deep 18cm tin for this recipe. This delicious Apple Shortcake will keep well in the fridge in an airtight container - that is, if you can resist not eating it all!

SHOPPING LIST...

450g cooking apples

3 level tsp sugar

110g butter

75g caster sugar

1 egg - *beaten*

175g self raising flour

pinch of salt

Lay two 28cm broad strips of baking parchment at right angles across the base and up the sides of an 18cm round cake tin. This will allow you to lift the shortcake out easily after cooking. Now line the base and sides with baking parchment.

Peel, core and slice the apples. Place them in a pan along with the sugar and barely enough water to cover. Simmer gently until cooked. Remove from the heat and allow them to cool.

Cream the butter and sugar together. Stir in the beaten egg before folding in the flour and salt and setting aside in the fridge for a few minutes to firm up.

Remove the batter from the fridge and divide it into two balls. Roll each piece into a 18cm round. Line the base of tin with one round, prick it all over with a fork and cover with the cooled apple, either randomly or in a pattern, whichever you prefer. Place the second round of shortbread on top of the apple and again prick lightly. Bake for 50 minutes - 1 hour at 325°F/170°C. To serve, sprinkle with a little caster sugar or enjoy warm with clotted cream.

CHEESY CAKES

—◦—

These tasty cheesy cakes make an excellent 'on the go' breakfast treat - try adding bacon and a sprinkle of spring onion for a different flavour.

SHOPPING LIST...

makes about 12

225g self raising flour

salt & pepper

½ tsp English mustard

110g butter

175g grated cheese

1 egg - *beaten with a little milk*

Grease a 12 hole bun tin, or an 18cm cake tin with a little butter.

Sift the flour, salt, pepper and English mustard together and rub in the butter. Stir in the cheese and bring the mixture together with the beaten egg, adding the milk slowly until you have enough to form a dough. Either knead into one large greased cake tin or separate into balls and fill a bun tin with each one.

Bake for 10-15 minutes at 375°F/190°C or until risen and golden brown.

Cool on a wire tray. Serve with butter and a selection of dips and houmous. Supermarket dips are absolutely brilliant – you can always place them in little dishes to give a more 'homemade' feel.

CHOCOLATE OATCAKES

So simple & so tasty! If preferred, swap the dark chocolate for white or milk chocolate.

SHOPPING LIST...

makes about 12

225g butter

175g dark soft brown sugar

225g porridge oats

25g hot chocolate or cocoa powder

For the topping:

225g plain dark chocolate

Grease a square 18cm shallow cake tin.

Slowly melt the butter in a saucepan over a low heat; remove from the heat and add the sugar, oats and hot chocolate or cocoa powder. Stir the mixture well before putting it into the tin. Flatten gently.

Bake at 350°F/180°C for approximately 15 minutes, or until it's bubbling. Remove from the oven and allow to cool.

To make the topping, melt the dark chocolate gently in a bowl over a saucepan of barely simmering (not boiling as this may 'cook' the chocolate causing it to spoil) hot water, then drizzle this glossy mixture onto the cooled oatcake.

Leave in a cool place until the chocolate is set. When the chocolate reaches a soft set, cut into 12 pieces (depending on the size you like).

CHRISTMAS CAKE

There are so many recipes for Christmas cake that I never know where to start. I like this recipe as it is one of the few that uses golden syrup – a flavour I find so warming and reminiscent of childhood puddings.

SHOPPING LIST...

450g sultanas
450g currants
112g raisins
112g dates - *lightly chopped*
110g Glacé cherries - *chopped*
50g almonds - *lightly chopped (optional)*
50g mixed peel
1 lemon* - *grated and juiced*
1 orange* - *grated and juiced*
275g butter
275g caster sugar
6 eggs - *beaten*
1 tbsp golden syrup
112g mixed spice
350g self raising flour
pinch of salt

Ideally, soak the fruit overnight the day before you wish to bake the cake. A good soaking allows the fruit to absorb the juice, making them extra plump, which ultimately ensures the cake is even more delicious. Don't worry if you haven't got time; a cake full of these ingredients can't do anything other than taste wonderful.

Double line a 25cm cake tin with baking parchment. In addition to lining the tin, I always tie a double sheet of brown paper around the outside of the tin as this stops the cake drying-out whilst cooking. Prepare two rounds of baking parchment for the top of the cake, each one with a hole cut in the middle to let the hot air escape.

Gather the dried fruit (sultanas, currants, raisins, dates, cherries, almonds - if using and mixed peel) in a large mixing bowl. Mix them together well before adding the rind and juice of the lemon and orange and again, stirring well. Cover and leave in a cool (but not cold) place overnight.

Cream the butter and sugar together. Add the beaten eggs, one at a time (don't worry if it curdles) and then add the remaining ingredients, including your now-blossoming fruit. Finally, fold-in the sifted flour (with the salt) gently so as not to lose any air. Place the mixture in the tin, flatten slightly and cover the top with your baking parchment rounds. Cook for 2 hours at 350°F/180°C and then reduce the oven to 300°F/150°C for a further 1 - 1½ hours. Test with a skewer to see if it's cooked. Allow to cool completely before removing it from the tin.

Remember to feed the cake at regular intervals between making and icing, and keep the cake well sealed in an air-tight container. About a week before Christmas, cover the top and sides with marzipan and royal icing.

The lemon and orange could be substituted for a wine-glass full of port or brandy or any other alcohol of your choice. Don't be afraid to use wine or cider – make your own tradition or try a different one each year. Variety is always a good idea!

COFFEE & WALNUT CAKE

Coffee cake is one of my favourites and can be made with or without walnuts. Simply leave them out if you don't wish to use them.

SHOPPING LIST...

4 tsp coffee granules or 1 shot espresso coffee

150g butter

150g caster sugar

2 large eggs - *beaten*

200g self raising flour

50g walnuts - *chopped*

For the icing:

1 tub American frosting

a few whole coffee beans or walnuts

Line two 20cm cake tins with baking parchment.

Make the coffee by mixing the coffee granules with 2 teaspoons of hot water from the kettle. Avoid using boiling water as this scalds the coffee which can make it slightly bitter. Alternatively, use a shot of espresso made as the instructions on your coffee-maker suggest.

Cream together the butter and sugar. Introduce the beaten eggs, one at a time and beat in the coffee. Now gently fold in the sifted flour, followed by the chopped walnuts. Divide between the two tins and bake for approximately 20-30 minutes at 350-375°F/180-190°C, or until a skewer comes out clean.

Ice with coffee frosting when completely cold. I like to use the instant American frosting you can buy in the supermarket (coffee or vanilla flavour – whichever catches my eye). It spreads easily and looks divine decorated with a few coffee beans or whole walnuts.

CUT & COME AGAIN CAKE

An easy recipe and a good standby in the cake tin. For a change, I sometimes use 110g dates in place of the fruit. The come again part is that this takes so little time to make, that it can almost come again while the first one cooks!

SHOPPING LIST...

110g butter

110g caster sugar

2 eggs - *beaten*

175g self raising flour

½ tsp baking powder

175g mixed dried fruit*

a little milk

*Mixed fruit:

sultanas, currants, raisins, mixed peel & Glacé cherries

Line a 18cm square cake tin with baking parchment.

Cream together the butter and sugar and then add the beaten eggs. Sift the flour and baking powder together before folding this into the creamed butter and sugar. Add the dried fruit and enough milk to make a fairly soft mixture.

Place this into the cake tin and bake for approximately 35-40 minutes at 350°F/180°C or until nicely brown and firm to the touch.

HEAVY CAKE

This delicious, traditional cake is perfect for picnics and goes so well with a nice cup of tea!

SHOPPING LIST...

110g lard or butter
450g flour
½ tsp salt
175g sugar
350g currants
approximately 120ml milk
110g butter
1 egg for glazing - *beaten*

Rub the lard or butter into the flour and add the salt, sugar and fruit. Mix to a soft dough with the milk. Turn on to a floured board and roll out to a long strip about 15cm wide.

Distribute half the butter in small pieces over the top two-thirds of the pastry. Fold the bottom third, without lard or butter, upwards and then the top third down over it.

Give the pastry a half turn so that the folds are at the sides. Roll out again into a thin strip and spread the rest of the butter as before, repeating the folding in the same way.

Roll out finally into a square about 1cm thick. Score the top into a lattice pattern, brush with egg and bake for about 30 minutes at 400°F/200°C.

LEMON SYRUP CAKE

An easy-peasy, lemon-squeezy cake to make that bursts with an amazing, zesty flavour.

SHOPPING LIST...

110g butter
175g caster sugar
2 lemons - *grated and juiced*
2 eggs - *beaten*
175g self raising flour
approximately 4 tbsp milk

For the lemon syrup:
juice from 2 lemons (above)
50g granulated sugar

Line a 900g loaf tin with baking parchment.

Cream the butter, caster sugar and lemon rind until fluffy, before adding each egg separately and beating well. Fold in the flour with approximately 4 tbsp milk. Add the mixture to the tin and smooth the top.

Bake for 45 - 50 minutes at 350-375°F/180-190°C or until firm, golden and shrinking from the sides of the tin.

Prepare the lemon syrup by heating the lemon juice and sugar gently until the sugar dissolves.

As soon as the cake comes out of the oven and while it's still in the tin, use a skewer to prick all over the top. Then pour the lemon syrup evenly over the cake.

Leave the cake in the tin until completely cold.

SYRUP CARROT CAKE

---◇---

One of my favourite cakes! Enjoy this delicious, iced, Syrup Carrot Cake with or without walnuts.

SHOPPING LIST...

175g butter
175g demerara sugar
75g golden syrup
275g self raising flour
pinch of salt
2 level tsp ground cinnamon
3 eggs - *beaten*
175g dates - *chopped*
225g finely grated carrots
2 rounded tbsp demerara sugar

For the icing:
soft cream cheese, lemon juice,
icing sugar & chopped walnuts
for decorating

Line a 20cm cake tin with baking parchment.

In a saucepan, slowly melt the butter, sugar and syrup together. Remove from the heat and sift in the flour, salt and cinnamon. Mix together well before adding the eggs, one at a time, stir in the dates and the grated carrot. Pour the batter into the tin, level off and sprinkle over the 2 tbsp of demerara sugar.

Bake the cake in the centre of the oven for 1 hour 40 minutes at 320°F/160°C. Test with a skewer; if it comes out clean and the cake is shrinking from the sides of the tin, it's cooked. It may need a little longer but do keep an eye on it. Leave to cool in the tin, then turn out and wrap in foil for 3-4 days to mature. When ready, cut the cake in half ready for icing.

For the icing: gently mix together enough soft cream cheese, lemon juice and icing sugar in a bowl. Using a palette knife, carefully spread the icing over the cake and decorate with the chopped walnuts.

APRICOT OAT CRUNCHIES • AUSTRALIAN CRUNCHIE • CHEESE SCONES • CHOCOLATE CRUMBLES • COCONUT SCRUNCHIES • FRUIT SCONES • FRUITY FLAPJACKS • GINGERBREAD • HOMEMADE TEACAKES • ICED FLAPJACKS • MELTING MOMENTS • NEW ZEALAND BISCUITS • NUTTY TOFFEE CRUNCH • OAT CRISPIES • SALTED CARAMEL SHORTIES • SHORTBREAD

BAKES

APRICOT OAT CRUNCHIES

———◇———

These really are so easy to make, a food processor will do the work for you if you prefer not to use your hands, and the crunchies keep wonderfully well in an airtight container.

SHOPPING LIST...

makes about 12

75g self raising wholemeal flour

75g granulated sugar

75g porridge oats

110g butter

110g dried apricots - *soaked overnight*

Optional topping:

coconut flakes

Line a swiss roll tin with baking parchment.

In a bowl mix together the flour, sugar and oats. Now rub in the butter until the ingredients resemble breadcrumbs.

Spread one half of the dough over the base of the tin and press down well. Drain and chop the apricots and sprinkle them over the mixture in the tin. Scatter the remaining mixture over the apricots and again, press down well. Bake for 25 minutes at 350°F/180°C or until golden brown.

Leave in the tin for about 1 hour or until cold. Cut into 12 pieces and serve.

Optional topping: sprinkle coconut flakes on top of the crunchies.

AUSTRALIAN CRUNCHIE

An irresistible tray bake, best served with a cup of tea!

SHOPPING LIST...

makes about 16

225g butter

150g caster sugar

75g coconut

60g cornflakes

150g plain flour

1 tbsp hot chocolate powder

For the icing:

175g icing sugar

1 level tbsp hot chocolate powder

a little hot water

Line a swiss roll tin with baking parchment.

Melt the butter over a low heat, then stir in the sugar, coconut, cornflakes, flour and hot chocolate powder. Mix gently but well. Turn the mixture into the tin, spreading it out into all four corners.

Bake for 30 minutes at 350-375°F/180-190°C.

While it's cooking, make the icing by mixing together the icing sugar, hot chocolate powder and a little hot water from the kettle. A thick coating consistency is perfect.

With the crunchie still hot from the oven, cover it entirely with the icing and leave until you have a soft set. At this point, mark out 16 squares (or less if you prefer bigger pieces) and leave until it's completely cold before removing from the tin.

CHEESE SCONES

I like to use a strong cheddar or stilton for this recipe but really any kind of cheese will work well.

SHOPPING LIST...

makes about 12

200g self raising flour

pinch of salt

½ tsp English mustard

40g butter

75g grated cheese + extra for the top

1 egg - *beaten with a little milk*

smoked paprika - *to sprinkle on top*

Line a tray with baking parchment.

Sift together the flour, salt and English mustard and rub in the butter. Stir in the grated cheese and enough egg and milk mixture to bring the dough together to form a soft (but not sticky) ball - be careful not to overwork the dough.

Roll out the dough to approximately 2cm in depth and either cut into squares (for a homemade look), or use a pastry cutter (for something slightly more perfect). Place on the baking parchment and add a small amount of grated cheese on top of each scone and a sprinkle of smoked paprika.

Bake for 10-15 minutes at 400°F/200°C.

CHOCOLATE CRUMBLES

---○---

A really straightforward and quick non-cook teatime treat. This is one of those recipes children could easily be asked to make.

SHOPPING LIST...

makes about 12

100g butter

2 tbsp golden syrup

25g caster sugar

4 tsp hot chocolate or cocoa powder

250g digestive biscuits

You will need an 18cm square shallow cake tin.

Melt the butter, golden syrup, sugar and hot chocolate or cocoa powder in a saucepan. Keeping the biscuits in their unopened packaging, gently crush them with a rolling pin. Now cut off one end and pour the crushed biscuits into the mixture and stir well.

Don't worry about uneven crushing, this will simply add greater texture to the Crumbles. Spread your lovely mixture into the cake tin and leave in the fridge to harden.

When set, cut into squares and serve with a cup of tea and a magazine or game.

COCONUT SCRUNCHIES

You will only need a few simple ingredients to make these delicious, quick & easy scrunchies. Indulge and enjoy the amazing mixture of textures and flavours this tray bake offers.

SHOPPING LIST...

makes about 12

110g butter

50g sugar

½ tbsp golden syrup

50g desiccated coconut

50g cornflakes

50g porridge oats

50g self raising flour

Line a swiss roll tin with baking parchment.

Melt the butter, sugar and golden syrup in a saucepan. Remove the pan from the heat and add the coconut, cornflakes, porridge oats and flour. Stir everything together carefully before pressing the mixture into the tin. Bake for 20 minutes at 350°F/180°C.

Once baked, cut into 12 squares and remove from the tin before it gets too cold.

FRUIT SCONES

Fruit scones make the perfect afternoon treat, best served with plently of jam and cream or butter.

SHOPPING LIST...

makes about 12

200g self raising flour

pinch of salt

40g butter

25g caster sugar

50g sultanas

1 egg - *beaten with a little milk*

Line a tray with baking parchment.

Sift together the flour and salt and rub in the butter. Mix in the sugar and the sultanas, before adding sufficient egg and milk to bring the mixture together. Roll out the dough, cut into scones either with a knife or a pastry cutter.

Place on the baking parchment and bake for approximately 10 minutes at 400°F/200°C.

Serve with clotted cream and jam, or a generous spread of butter.

FRUITY FLAPJACKS

———◇———

A colourful, fruity twist on a classic British bake. I love a piece of flapjack and with the dried fruit, cherries and apple, this recipe is even more delicious.

SHOPPING LIST...

makes about 12

85g soft butter

25g soft brown sugar

2 tbsp golden syrup

1 tbsp black treacle

175g porridge oats

75g mixed dried fruit*

8 Glacé cherries - *cut into quarters*

1 apple - *thinly sliced*

*Mixed fruit:

raisins, sultanas, currants

Line a swiss roll tin with baking parchment.

Add the butter, sugar, golden syrup and black treacle to a pan and heat gently until melted together.

Add the oats, fruit and cherries and stir well until everything is evenly coated. Place half of the mixture into the tin and press down firmly.

Cover this with a layer of sliced apple and add the rest of the mixture on top of the apple. Smooth out. Cook for 20-30 minutes at 375°F/190°C.

Cut into fingers while still warm and remove from the tin when cold.

GINGERBREAD

This cake is so good for freezing. I usually make the whole amount, cut the cake in half when cold and freeze one half. It's especially useful for emergencies as it defrosts very quickly and can be either a cake or a pudding. If the latter, serve with clotted cream for an extra-special treat!

SHOPPING LIST...

100g butter

100g light soft brown sugar

100g golden syrup

75g black treacle

150ml milk

200g plain flour

4 tsp ground ginger

1 tsp bicarbonate soda

1 egg - *beaten*

Line a 20cm square cake tin with baking parchment.

Melt the butter, sugar, golden syrup, black treacle and milk over a low heat. Cool the mixture until lukewarm. Sift together the flour, ground ginger and bicarbonate of soda and add this, with the egg, to the cooled liquid. Stir well.

Pour the mixture into the prepared tin and bake for approximately 1-1½ hours at 300°F/150°C, or until the gingerbread springs back when pressed gently.

HOMEMADE TEACAKES

These homemade teacakes are absolutely delicious toasted with lashings of salted butter.

SHOPPING LIST...

makes about 6

500g strong plain flour

50g caster sugar

pinch of salt

1 sachet dried yeast

50g butter

250ml milk - *warmed slightly*

100g sultanas*

100g raisins*

milk to glaze

*I know some people like to soak their fruit in tea overnight. While it isn't necessary for this recipe, if you have time, it does add a little extra to the flavours. Simply make a pot of tea the evening before, pour an extra cup (around 100ml of strong, black tea) and add the fruit to it before leaving them to soak overnight.

Sift the flour, caster sugar, salt and yeast into a bowl and rub in the butter. Gradually pour in enough milk to bring the dough together. When you have a soft but not sticky dough, turn it out onto a floured work surface and knead it well for around 10 minutes or until it is beautifully smooth and elastic in texture.

Place the dough into a clean bowl and cover it with a tea towel. Leave both to stand in a warm (but not hot) place until the dough has doubled in size. At this point, add the sultanas and raisins and knead them into the dough until they are evenly spread. Divide the dough into six large teacakes, shaping each one into a round ball before pressing down or rolling out to about the same size as the top of a mug. Place on a tray, lined with baking parchment, leaving plenty of room for growth. Cover with a sheet of baking parchment and leave until they have doubled in size.

Brush each teacake with the milk and bake at 350°F/180°C for 12-16 minutes. Eat straight away with plenty of butter or save until the next day when they will toast beautifully!

ICED FLAPJACKS

———◦———

This is best cooked in a square cake tin, as it makes it easier to cut up. It does rise considerably, so you will need a large tin.

SHOPPING LIST...

makes about 12

125g butter

75g demerara sugar

50g golden syrup

200g porridge oats

For the icing:

1 tbsp instant coffee - *mixed with cold water*

hot water

100g icing sugar

Line a square cake tin with baking parchment.

Melt the butter, sugar and golden syrup over a low heat before adding the porridge oats, stir well.

Spread the mixture evenly into the lined tin and bake for 20 minutes at 375-425°F/190-220°C. Leave in the tray to cool down, ready to ice.

To make the icing, mix together the instant coffee with 2 teaspoons of hot water from the kettle. Add enough coffee to the icing sugar to make a good covering.

When the flapjacks are cool, pour over the icing and tilt the tray to spread it out. Leave to set before cutting into squares.

MELTING MOMENTS

A classic recipe, these delicious melt-in-the-mouth biscuits are made using just a few simple ingredients and are great fun for the children to bake.

SHOPPING LIST...

makes about 16

150g butter

150g caster sugar

1 tsp vanilla essence

1 egg - *beaten*

275g self raising flour

150g cornflakes - *crushed*

Glacé cherries for decoration

Line a tray with baking parchment.

Beat the butter to a cream before adding the sugar and vanilla essence and beating further until light and creamy. Add the egg and the sifted flour to make a fairly firm consistency. Roll the mixture into 16 balls.

Roll each ball in the crushed cornflakes and place on the baking parchment, allowing a good space between each one. Flatten slightly and press ½ a Glacé cherry into each biscuit.

Bake for 15-20 minutes at 350-375°F/180-190°C.

NEW ZEALAND BISCUITS

———○———

These appear to be quite fiddly but in fact they are very easy. The combination of porridge oats and coconut make them very well-behaved when you're shaping them.

SHOPPING LIST...

makes about 30

150g butter

110g caster sugar

1 heaped tbsp golden syrup

110g plain flour

75g porridge oats

50g desiccated coconut

2 level tsp bicarbonate soda

Line a tray with baking parchment.

Melt the butter, sugar and golden syrup in a pan over a low heat. Stir in the plain flour, porridge oats and desiccated coconut. Dissolve the bicarbonate soda in 1 tbsp of hot water and stir this into the coconut mixture. Leave to cool for a few minutes and then divide into 30 portions.

Roll each one into a ball and place on the baking parchment. If you prefer, you could always place a spoon full of the mixture on the baking sheet and flatten it slightly with the back of a spoon.

Bake for 20 minutes at 325°F/170°C, or until golden.

NUTTY TOFFEE CRUNCH

This seriously nutty recipe is for nut eaters ONLY. This delicious crunch is so versatile, with so many different types of nut to choose from, you can use what ever you like!

SHOPPING LIST...

85g mixed nuts*
85g caster sugar
60ml water

*Mixed nuts:
. use a good selection of nuts
for your crunch, you could
try; *pecans, walnuts, almonds,
hazelnuts, cashews & peanuts*

Line a tray with baking parchment.

Roast the mixed nuts under the grill until just brown. Into a heavy-based saucepan, place the water and sugar and heat slowly without stirring until the sugar has dissolved.

Bring this to the boil, before adding the nuts and boiling rapidly until the mixture turns a rich brown colour.

Tip the mixture quickly onto the baking parchment and leave to set. When cold, break into pieces and store in an airtight container.

OAT CRISPIES

These tasty little Oat Crispies are super quick & easy to make and they make the perfect energy snack.

SHOPPING LIST...

100g butter
75g caster sugar
1 tsp golden syrup
3 tsp boiling water
50g porridge oats
110g self raising flour
½ level tsp baking powder
vanilla essence

Line a tray with baking parchment.

Cream the butter with the caster sugar and add the golden syrup and boiling water. Stir well before adding the porridge oats, self raising flour, baking powder and a few drops of vanilla essence.

Roll the mixture into balls, place on the baking parchment allowing for growth during cooking.

Bake at 350-375°F/180-190°C for approximately 15-20 minutes.

Optional topping: melt 200g of salted caramel chocolate in a bowl over a pan of barely simmering water. When melted, either add a teaspoon full to each or the shorties or drizzle the over each one. The chocolate should harden quickly so you can eat them very soon!

SALTED CARAMEL SHORTIES

—◦—

SHOPPING LIST...

makes about 18

For the caramel:

75g golden caster sugar

15g salt flakes

For the shortbread:

125g plain flour

75g soft brown sugar

110g butter

Line two trays with baking parchment or use the same one twice.

For the caramel: gently heat the sugar until melted in a heavy-based saucepan, stirring frequently and making sure it doesn't 'catch' and burn. Continue heating gently until the sugar takes on a dark, glossy colour and texture. At this point, remove it from the heat, add the salt flakes and give a final stir. Now pour this sugar and salt mixture onto the lined tray, tilt to make sure it reaches all the corners and leave it to set. Once completely cold, break the caramel into small pieces and set aside.

Note: Care must be taken when heating sugar as it boils at a far higher temperature (around 320°F/160°C) than water (200°F/100°C) and can spit.

For the shortbread: sift the flour and sugar together into a bowl and rub in the butter. Gently knead in the caramel pieces until they are evenly distributed. Turn the caramel dough onto a floured board and divide into 18 pieces. Roll each piece into a ball, place them onto the baking parchment and flatten slightly.

Bake for 15 minutes at 350-375°F/180-190°C. Leave to cool.

SHORTBREAD

An irresistible buttery, crumbly biscuit. This recipe is so easy to follow and will go perfect with a cup of tea or coffee.

SHOPPING LIST...

makes about 10

300g plain flour

pinch of salt

200g butter

50g caster sugar + extra for sprinkling

Line a tray with baking parchment.

Sift the flour into a basin with a pinch of salt and rub in the butter. When the mixture resembles breadcrumbs add the sugar and knead the mixture into a ball (add a little cold water if necessary).

Cut the dough in half and form (with your hands for an informal look, or with a rolling pin for a more structured one) each piece into a sqaure and place on the lined tray.

Bake for 12 minutes at 300-320°F/150-160°C until pale golden. Cool on a wire tray and to serve, sprinkle with caster sugar.

AUTUMN APPLE TART • BAKEWELL TART • BREAD PUDDING
• GOLDEN APPLE PUDDING • MINI RASPBERRY MERINGUES
• STRAWBERRY CAKE • SUMMER PUDDING • TREACLE TART

PUDDINGS

AUTUMN APPLE TART

We all enjoy a traditional mincemeat tart at Christmas, however this recipe is great for those of you who like a slightly less sweet dish.

SHOPPING LIST...

For the pastry:
50g butter
110g plain flour
1 egg - *beaten*

For the filling:
1 cooking apple - *cored, peeled & sliced*
150g mincemeat

Line a 20cm flan tin with baking parchment.

Make the pastry by rubbing the butter into the flour until it resembles breadcrumbs. Add enough egg to bring the pastry together and chill for 20 minutes.

Divide the pastry into two and roll out each half to the same size as the tin.

To help balance the sweetness, line your tin with pastry as usual, then spread with a thin layer of mincemeat and cover this with a layer of sliced cooking apple.

Top with a further layer of pastry and bake at 350-375°F/180-190°C for approximately 30 minutes.

BAKEWELL TART

To make this popular tart even more delicious, add flaked almonds, whole raspberries or redcurrants on top of the mixture before placing it in the oven to bake.

SHOPPING LIST...

For the pastry:
50g butter
110g plain flour
1 egg - *beaten*

For the filling:
50g butter
50g sugar
50g semolina
1 tsp almond essence
1 egg - *beaten*
½ tsp baking powder
2 tbsp raspberry jam

Line a 20cm deep greased sandwich tin with baking parchment.

Make up the pastry, as for Autumn Apple Tart (page 66), and line the tin. Spread the jam evenly over the pastry.

For the filling: melt the butter and sugar in a saucepan and stir in the semolina, cook for a few minutes stirring all the time.

Remove from the heat, cool a little and add the almond essence, stir well. Mix together the baking powder and the beaten egg before adding to the almond mixture.

Pour the filling over the jam, covering all the edges. Bake at 350-375°F/180-190°C for 25-30 minutes.

BREAD PUDDING

—◦—

This Bread Pudding recipe is so easy to make, using leftover bread and a few simple ingredients. It's delicious served warm with a nice big scoop of ice cream!

SHOPPING LIST...

500g stale white & brown bread
300ml milk
125g sultanas
125g raisins
2 tsp nutmeg
2 tsp cinnamon + extra for sprinkling
2 tsp ginger
1 tsp vanilla extract
1 large egg - *beaten*
140g caster sugar + extra for sprinkling
100g butter

Line a 20cm square cake tin with baking parchment and preheat the oven to 350°F/180°C.

Tear or chop the white & brown bread into pieces, place into a large mixing bowl and cover with the milk. Leave the mixture to soak for approximately 30 minutes. Mix together adding the fruit, spices and vanilla extract. Then add the large beaten egg and the caster sugar. Chop the butter into small pieces and add to the pudding mixture, stir well with a wooden spoon or use your hands to mix.

Pour the mixture evenly into the lined cake tin. Sprinkle a little extra caster sugar and cinnamon over the top and bake for 1-2 hours until firm and golden.

Cut into pieces and serve warm. For an extra special treat, serve with some delicious vanilla ice cream.

GOLDEN APPLE PUDDING

Simply delicious! This Golden Apple Pudding really does smell & taste amazing. Indulge while still warm with custard or cream.

SHOPPING LIST...

For the pudding:

110g self raising flour

50g suet or vegetarian alternative

pinch of salt

cold water to mix

For the filling:

100g golden syrup

1 medium sized apple - *chopped finely*

custard or cream for serving

Grease a 450ml basin with butter.

Mix together the self raising flour, suet and the pinch of salt in a bowl, then add enough cold water to make a soft dough. Divide the dough into two and place one half in the bottom of the basin. Cover with 50g of golden syrup.

Put the chopped apple on top of the mixture, then add the 50g of remaining golden syrup and finally top with the rest of the dough.

Cover with greased foil and place in a saucepan with a lid. Add enough water to sit half-way up the bowl and bring to the boil. Simmer for 1½ hours. Do not allow to boil dry.

Serve with lashings of custard, or double cream.

MINI RASPBERRY MERINGUES

———◦———

A fantastically quick & easy pudding to make and a perfect treat for those hot summer evenings.

SHOPPING LIST...

450g clotted cream

8 mini meringue nests

8 raspberries - *per meringue nest*

fresh mint - *washed and spun in a salad spinner*

Place one tablespoon of the clotted cream into each meringue nest. Cover with the raspberries and place a mint leaf on the top of each one.

You may wish to sprinkle icing sugar over the top of each meringue just before serving.

Note: these nests work equally well with blueberries, blackcurrants, strawberries, blackberries, in fact, just about any fruit!

Farm Fresh
EGGS

STRAWBERRY CAKE

Here is a very easy recipe and one of the tastiest ways to serve strawberries.

SHOPPING LIST...

For the sponge:

3 eggs

75g caster sugar

1 tbsp hot water

75g plain flour

For the cake mixture:

2 tbsp caster sugar

450g strawberries

300ml carton of double cream

With a little butter, grease a swiss roll tin.

Make a whisked sponge by mixing together the eggs, caster sugar and hot water, before folding in the plain flour. Pour the sponge mixture into the tin and tap the sides gently to even it out. Bake at 375°F/190°C for approximately 12-15 minutes.

Turn out and allow to cool. This can be made beforehand and frozen.

Sprinkle the caster sugar over the strawberries and leave in the fridge until needed. Take a 300ml carton of double cream and whip gently until it holds its shape.

Cut the cake in half (cross-wise), spread one half with the cream, then scatter some of the strawberries over. Place the other half of the sponge on top, then add the cream and decorate using the remaining strawberries. Place in the fridge for 1-2 hours to settle before serving.

SUMMER PUDDING

Choose a variety of fruit, the more you have, the more interesting and colourful the Summer Pudding.

SHOPPING LIST...

8 slices of white bread - *crusts removed*

900g summer fruits*

110g sugar

cream for serving

*Summer fruits:
strawberries, raspberries, gooseberries, blueberries. red & black currants, rhubarb, blackberries or any available fruits

Line a 1.2 litre pudding basin with slices of white bread, cutting a round for the bottom.

Cook your choice of summer fruits in a saucepan with the sugar and a little water until softened but not broken up.

Fill the lined basin with the fruit, top with bread and cover with a saucer or small plate with a weight on top.

Chill in the fridge for several hours. Turn out just before serving and spoon extra fruit over the top.

Serve with cream.

TREACLE TART

One of my all time favourites, delicious warmed and served with vanilla ice cream.

SHOPPING LIST...

225g shortcrust pastry
1 large cooking apple
4 tbsp golden syrup
110g fresh white breadcrumbs

Line a 20cm flan tin with baking parchment.

Roll the pastry so that it is larger than the flan tin. Place the rolling pin in the middle of your pastry circle and gently wrap the pastry around so that it can be easily moved. Place on top of the lined tin and using your hands, press the pastry into the edges, remembering to leave a slight overhang - this can be trimmed later.

Peel, core and slice the apple and place on the pastry.

Mix the syrup and breadcrumbs and pour over the apple. Decorate with pastry trimmings in a lattice pattern.

Bake for 45 minutes at 400°F/200°C until golden.

When out of the oven, using a small sharp knife, carefully cut the overhang pastry off the tart. Leave to cool and cut into slices. This tart can be easily warmed and tastes great with a nice big scoop of ice cream.

NOTES

NOTES